Life Is

a Team

Game

By. Jerrell Gooden

ISBN 978-0-578-69608-9 (paperback)

jerrellg6@gmail.com

Table of

Contents

Overview

<u>Overview</u>

This book is about teamwork in this game called life. Life can be peaceful, but it can also be chaotic and stressful if you let it. Life has its up and downs, and it can also be depending on the situation that you're in rather good or bad. In my opinion in order to make it where you want to be you have to learn how to work well with others and share ideas. Well, what I am getting at is that being a team player might be the best approach when dealing with life in general.

Everyone needs somebody to help them get through the rough times and rise to the top and stay up there. When people work together as a unit life can be a whole lot easier especially if the team has a common goal to be accomplished. Teamwork is the key to life no matter what you are doing. When you have good teammates and you all are on the same page you can accomplish anything that you set your mind to. I also will be talking about how a team that is divided cannot stand. So, for the people who will be reading this book I hope it helps you in life, because everyone will eventually need help one way, or another in this game of life.

Chapter 1

Learning the true

meaning of the word Team

The word team is defined a group of players forming one side in a competitive game or sport. In order to work together as a team, you will have to know and have a clear understand of the word. Sometimes the word team can be misused, for example the saying, take one for the team. That saying can get you into a situation that may be difficult to get out of, I mean if you can get out of it at all. In life there is a lot of peer pressure that the word team is involved.

Being there for one another in life no matter what you are doing is the key. Teams are not formed overnight. It takes time for everyone to learn how to work together in life instead of belittling the next person or looking down on them. No matter what you do as a team with a common goal in life don't act like you're above your teammates because without someone or people helping you, you won't get very far in life by being a selfish teammate. Being loyal to your teammate even if you all are on bad terms is a must, especially if there is a common goal to be dealt with.

Another way how I would define the word team would be family. The reason why I choose family is because that's one of the first teams in life that you start off with. In my book, without your family all them other teams in life won't have your back like they do. Loyalty doesn't need to change just because of a disagreement that you may have on the way things are going.

In addition to defining the word team would be helping people when sometimes you don't want to, but in God's eyes it's the right thing to do. I'm not saying let people use you but however, make sure that you are doing it out of love. I recall a time that a friend of mine was behind on his schoolwork and it took the entire class to catch him up. Each classmate helped him with one worksheet, and he was caught up again.

Team is just like a family or your brothers and sisters. I also recall my mother telling me about she had to help her siblings get ready for school and sometimes worked out in the field to help my grandmother with the bill. She was one of the oldest and according to what she told me that came with a lot of responsibility. Trust me she told me a lot of stories when it came to teamwork. If you have a family that sticks together, you can accomplish anything that is difficult.

When you or when you have a person that has that team first mentality the sky's the limit. Sometimes one toxic person can divide a team or break a unit if you let them. In some cases, that is why you must get rid of them and part ways. Sometimes it may be hard, but you must do what best for the team, and I am not talking about just sports either. A perfect example of this would be at a job when a coworker is being disruptive in an inappropriate way. He or she has been warned numerous times, I mean I am a strong believer in second chances but when it comes down rather you or the team want to accomplish a common goal that's when self-preservation comes in.

Being there for one another as a team is particularly important in my book even with the times are rough and rocky. Like I said before you really find out about your team when times get hard as well as your friendship. Another thing that I said before was when a person is being a part of the problem and not the solution, that can destroy a team from within.

I recall a time while I was in college and we had a project that was due. Each member of our group had a certain job to do. We made sure that everybody had a part in the project as in getting involved so we can get a passing grade. At the end of the day we all passed and when got an A for the project. The moral of the story is to get everyone involved and does let a person just sit back and not do anything to contribute to the group.

It is easy in life when times and everything are going great, but when things get rough your team is either going to fall apart or stick together. It is like my mom always told me and my siblings, together we stand divided we fall. You win as a team and you lose as a team. It is just like in football one person makes a mistake the whole team suffers.

Defining the word team in my own words can be hard especially when a person feels like they do not need their team anymore. Some people forget that it is a team effort to get where you are in life and get the big head. In the long run that can and will come back to haunt you one day and you will be searching for the people that helped get you where you are today. It is especially important to thank your team always, because without help, you will not get very

far in life.

Chapter 2

Learning in life we are

all in this together

A person with a team first mentality is a plus. That means that he or she is willing to work as a team for a common goal. A person's individual goals and accolades do not matter to them as long as the common goal is accomplished. People of course care about individual goals, but a good team player wants to win first then worry about them things.

In life, we are all in this together. Learning to help one another without expecting anything in return is a good mentality to have in God's eyes. I once heard an old story out the bible about people doing for others to please people. God says do your good deed in secret. God also says that do not let your left hand know what your right hand is doing. To be real, if a person that is doing something for me and they really don't what to do it then I much rather you not do it for me at all if I was to be talked about after a person did it for me.

One way to make a good team is listening to one another. Communication is the key in life because without it there is extraordinarily little your team can do. In my opinion everyone needs a person to hear them out.

Hearing a person out an acting accordingly is one of the crucial components that you and your team will need in the long run. You do not have to yell, swear, or get into a shouting match to get your point across either, that's sometimes can cause a team to divide and crumble.

Life is a Team Game

Listening to another person's ideas can be a tall order sometimes. The reason is because some people are closed minded. Being closed minded about everything is not going to get you anywhere in life. Working with other people even if you don't get along with them can be a tall order to. They may have good ideas, but in order to make them work, you have got to swallow your pride sometimes. The more ideas you share the better off we will be. There is a lot to learn about sharing ideas with others.

Listening to other people point of views can be a good thing. Anybody can help in a current situation that you may be in. Even a little kid can tell you something that we may be doing right or wrong. We cannot let pride and selfishness get in the way of a common goal that you and the people that you encounter get in the way. Pride can be used in a good or bad way. In addition to that would be we often refuse to work with an enemy or just a person for whatever reason. The more we work as a team, the better off you will be, and life will be easy a little bit.

To be real about it, life is hard enough as it is. I often ask myself this question, "Why did Adam and Eve eat that fruit that God told them not to eat?" I realize now more than ever that everything happens for a reason and it was a part of God's plan all along. The way I look at it would be that God has a plan for all of us, and he expects us to work as a team in this game of life to get to heaven. The whole point of me saying what I just said about Adam and Eve is we all have a job to do in life and it's going to take a team effort to achieve our common goal. Don't let the word pride get in the way, because you may miss out on the award in the end.

Life is a Team Game

Trying new ideas can be a risky thing to do especially if when you're scared. For example, I was scared to get my driver's license when I was younger. The outcome of my situation was not getting a car until I was 28 years old, but I am glad I got them now. I was afraid to ask people to help me because the fear of either failing or being yelled at got in the way. Despite all that, I overcame my fear and got what I needed and sometimes it takes courage to ask for help in a critical situation that I was in.

Like is said before trying new ideas can be risky, but in my opinion, it may be the best way to go. I think that trying new ideas as a team can be good. Agreeing on an idea as a team is particularly important, I mean it keeps the team together as a whole no matter what the outcome may be. New ideas can also be scary to try, but no matter what the outcome it all a team effort is to get a common goal accomplished.

Others may disagree with the decision about new ideas to try, but life is not perfect. Sometimes you must get along in a group to accomplish a common goal. Trying new ideas to make things easier in life can be better for all parties that are involved rather it is a business dilemma or sport team etc.

When you have a small business, it takes a team effort to keep it running. You may have to put your pride aside to achieve the task at have, but at the end of the day the goal can be achieved. It is like that old saying all for one and one for all.

New ideas can come from anywhere from coworkers and the main people that or in charge of the situation. Just because an idea sounds good on paper doesn't mean it is when it comes to a life situation that you or the people that you may come in contact with, that's why they are called ideas. In my opinion, new ideas should be shared among the group so you all can be on the same page about certain things.

In this game of life, we are all in it together. No one is better than the next person. That is why we work together to achieve common goals whatever they may be. Listening to one another, sharing, and trying new ideas can three of the best assets to have in your corner. Some people may want to be on their own and that can be good to however, in life when you need help don't let your pride get in the way of things you may want to achieve that you can't do on your own.

You may have a term paper that is due for example, but you did all your work at school and you cannot save it because you don't have a flash drive. You too afraid you ask a friend or a family member for one. This is another example how some people let pride get in the way of a situation that is especially important when it involves your grades. Do not let it happen otherwise you may miss out on passing that class and you fail because you did not ask for help in a situation that could have been avoided.

The moral of the example I just used would be do not be afraid to ask for help when you need it. Believe it or not I had to learn this myself the hard way when I was trying to pass this accounting class in college. In the end I went to get help and it was one of the best decisions I have made in college while I was there at the time.

Working together in life can make it easier on you and the person or group that you are in contact with. For your life to be a little easier, you have to be willing and have the will power to be a team player in certain situations that come up. Everybody needs someone to get through the ups and downs that life has to offer. Sharing ideas and agreeing to work together in certain situations is a must if you want life to be a little easier. Your trust in people is also tested in the people that you come in contact or working with to accomplish a common goal.

Chapter 3

Chemistry in Life

In order to have good chemistry in life with the people you come in contact or work with you must get to know one another. When I started at SRG global Inc., I was shy at first and a loner. When I got to know people that is when my life started to change. Do not get me wrong I am still a little shy, but it took me a while to get out of it and it is a working progress for me. To be honest I do not know where I got my shyness from. It is never a dull moment at the job I work at, and I try to have the best day possible while working there and still learning new things about people and everything else. The true meaning of chemistry would be the complex emotional or psychological interaction between two people. The meaning in my own words would be having a bond and a natural outlook on certain things that comes the groups way in life. Learning about one another is a must if you want to achieve a common goal with someone. It is like I said before everybody is going to need help at some point in life especially in hard situations that life has to offer.

Having a good chemistry with someone is a major asset if you want your life to be a little easier. One of the ways to learn about a person is to hang out with them a little bit. They say that first impressions are everything, but to be honest it is not. When you first meet someone, they might be having a bad and do not feel like talking to anyone. People do not know what others go through in life, so you cannot just judge a person to be bad, but we often do.

From personal experience, I have seen people that were enemies have exceptionally good chemistry in the things that involves a group effort. It's like that old saying sometimes in order to go along you have to get along even if it is a person that you don't really care for, but at the same time you both have a common critical goal to maintain. Working with an enemy or a person that you don't really care for can be a challenge, but there are many ways to still be a team player in certain situations in life.

I recall a time when I was in junior high that I had to play basketball with players on the team that I did not really care for. We may have not got along, but we manage to have a winning season none the less. I guess my point is that sometimes you must go with the flow even if It's hard working with someone that you don't like or care for. In addition to what I just said would be for example if a person that you don't really care for in life was in some kind of need and they came to you, help them out with no questions asked. It's like the Bible says, do good to people that mistreat you and pray for them.

Learning about one another can be hard sometimes, but in order to have good chemistry you will have to do that. Before a group is formed, all the parties must learn about each other. I remember when I was in grade school, I hated to split up into groups. Remember back in the day I recalled being a loner and believe in doing my own work by myself. My teachers told me to give it some time and you like working and interacting with other kids. My teachers turned out to be right in the end especially on complicated things I could not figure out on my own.

Working together and having great chemistry in life with that person or group of people rather friend or foe can really get you where you need and want to be in life. To be honest, I believe that it could be poetry in motion. You may not like it sometimes but working together in groups can get a lot done regardless of what the goals are.

Everybody needs help occasionally, that's why I believe that it is important to get to know people and develop a good professional relationship with them. Chemistry with a person that has the same common goal as you can get the both of you in a good place in life if you put your mind to it. The true definition of the word chemistry is the complex emotional or psychological interaction between two people. Psychology has a lot to do with the chemistry between two or more people. You can be a rival to another person and still have good chemistry with someone.

I have seen fellow rivals have good chemistry in the WWE. The reason why I used the WWE as an example, because when you watch a match you see two people working together to make the match good. The people that watch the WWE, it is also poetry in motion when two combatants are in the ring cooperating with each other to put on a great show and also making sure that the moves that they put on each other are safe ones.

Working with someone in life that you do not have good chemistry with can be a bad thing sometimes especially if all they do is complain about the situation all the time. That is another thing that we must watch out for. You can have bad chemistry with someone in life that is not a team player. Some people don't want to work as a team to achieve a common goal sometimes. If you are not going to be a team player in my opinion, you are part of the problem and not the solution. Getting along with your teammates or the group that you are in is a must. You do not have to like each other in order to achieve common goals that life throws at you, but you just must have respect for one another.

In addition to having good chemistry in the things that need to be done as a team or group would be you have to know the likes and dislikes about certain things when it comes to accomplishing a certain goal that is at hand. Knowing your group or team's likes and dislikes about the things is especially important. You're not going to always like the things that your group may do, however in order to have in understanding about them things you will have to talk about them instead of being quiet about the dislikes

you or the group might have as a whole.

I have personally seen groups or teams divide

or disintegrate over either a disagreement or

something that an individual had said in a group that

may have offended someone else. I am not saying that

you must agree with the things that your group have

to say or do all the time. It is like the old saying goes,

a close mouth does not get feed, and there is a lot of

trust to that statement. I can recall being the quiet and

shy type while I was in school. A lot of things I

should have spoken up for I did not because the fact

of being afraid that my opinion did not matter. I

learned later in life to remain steadfast and have a

little more courage. Sometimes having a little courage

can be a good thing to have. My mother taught me at

a young age to stand up for what is right and have

courage behind what you say by being careful with the words you chose.

Another way to keep good chemistry with someone or a good would be having an open mind about each other's ideas. There is different way to be doing that. Being negative about a person's idea is not the way to be, you got to have an open mind about the things that they say. I heard many times when a person has an idea to make the situation better you always have someone in the group that is always negative. Sometimes certain people do not have an open mind about someone's ideas and that is not ok. A negative person in a group can be poison.

Having an open mind about ideas and having good chemistry can go hand in hand. The reason why I say that is because when you have an open mind and not being negative about someone's ideas that can create great chemistry within the entire group or team that you are involved in life. Life is about taking chances sometimes and they may be for the best. Sometimes, the chances you take can be good or bad.

Everyone has different ideas sometimes when it comes to either working as a team or just with another party. Learning to have respect for another person's ideas is especially important. Sometimes another person's ideas can be the make or break of the situation so choose wisely. You cannot be closeminded about certain ideas all the time even if they're not logical. My mom always told me to have an open mind about any situation and another person's ideas before you jump to conclusions. Jumping to conclusions so quick without thinking about certain situations can really mess your team or group up in the long run.

I never could really grasp on what my mom was trying to say about having an open mind until I got old enough to understand. All these years later I am finally seeing what she was talking about. Well what I am getting at is listening to someone that is older and have been through the situation or goal that you are trying to achieve is important.

By having an open mind, you can judge the situation and act on it accordingly. Some ideas may sound good on paper but, they can be a problem in the future if not handle or used in a correct way. Do not ever try to down a person when they come up with an idea. Downing and belittling people is not going to get your goals or situations accomplished, nor will help the team. Like I said before, it is important to have an open mind about every idea and act accordingly.

<u>Chapter 4</u>

Staying together

You may have heard the saying all for one and one for all, and there is a lot of truth to that statement. The reason that it is the truth is because when you are working together in life and everyone is a team player it makes things so much better no matter what you're trying to accomplish. Being a team player and staying together during the good and bad times is an exceptionally good way to prove that you're loyal especially during the bad times. I have seen first-hand teams and groups split up on account of either a misunderstanding or just the times got hard. God said in the Bible no matter what never lose your faith in yourself or a person, but he knows our hearts and we do fall short sometimes. God also says no matter what praise him in the good and bad times.

Your loyalty and faith get tested every day, it is just how you keep it and get through the situation together. It is easy to say you are loyal and all about the team or group when everything is going right, however when times get rough and hard then that is when your loyalty and team first mentality get put to the test. I have seen some of the best team or groups fall apart just because times get hard. That is why it is important to stay together and fight through adversity.

Everyone goes through adversity in life there is no way around it. There are stories about athletes that go through it. Some people's struggles are worse than others. I see people judge others about their current situation, but at the same time we should not do that because you never know what is behind it.

Life is a Team Game

Even myself got judged by certain people because I lived with my mother. Me and my sister and bothers had to work together to take care of our mother and I never regret doing it because some kids do not even think about their parents when they are sick. Me and my siblings may have had differences, but at the end of the day that was still our mom and we did what we needed to do to take care of her and we worked as a team doing it.

Sometimes groups disband just because it gets too hard. When it gets hard and intense, that is when you find out about your team or group that you are in. That is why it takes will power and mental toughness to survive in life when you are working together. When you work together life is so much easier. the key to life when you are working as a team is learning the concept of winning and losing together.

Hard times do not last forever but however, when your team or group has a hard time getting along and coming to an agreement it can make the situation or goal much harder to achieve. This game of life does not get any easier but it is how you look at every situation and realize that it doesn't have to be hard all the time. Faith in your teammates rather it involves playing sports or just working in a group is a major asset that you want to have, because without it you are not going to get anything done. You also need to realize that God is in control of everything in life.

A lot of people think that the people that are rich or wealthy do not have any problems. Even though they do not have financial issues does not mean the game of life cannot be hard for them. Most of the people that are rich had to work as a team to get where they are at today, they did not do it by themselves. It is just like them famous inventors, if they kept it all to themselves, we would have never been able to enjoy the things that we have today.

It is like I said in the last chapter, in order to work together to achieve a common goal you must have great chemistry with one another. Getting through the bad times and disagreements is a must. I used to hate getting in groups as a little kid in school because I felt like I was about business and some of the people was not. Never try to get in a group or on a team that wants to reap the rewards when they never contributed to the group.

Sometimes it can be hard to praise God in the bad times. It also takes a lot of mental toughness for a team to stay together. When things are going ok all the time it is easy to say that you got your teammate's back and all that. Your toughness and faith in God as well as your will gets tested when things are not going so well. Reaching down to find that inner strength and evaluating yourself on what you are doing wrong can be a tall order sometimes. Some people let pride get in the way of the team goals. We all must learn that the word pride can get you into some messed up situations that you or your team cannot get out of. Even if you do not like your teammate or the group that you are in, do not let the word pride get in the way. You do not have to like each other but you will have to respect one another for the task at have can be achieved.

Giving the Lord the praise is a must rather the situation or the times are good or bad. God is in control of every situation. I recall times when I was playing football in high school that the team and the coaches prayed before every game and after. Looking back on it now I was forever grateful that we made

that a habit even after practice. Keeping your faith

that God will help you and the team in hard times is a

must.

　　With God all things are possible, we should

not let anyone else tell us any different. Many teams

fall apart when God isn't present in their lives,

however the strongest teams survive because the good

Lord is praised in every good or bad situation and the

faith is kept that God is going to get the job done

regardless how deep a whole that you and your team

is in. Bad times do not last forever, but how long they

last can also depend on the situation that the team or

group is in or either their stubbornness not to trust

God in the bad times. Do not ever be ashamed to say

to your group that God is in control and will get the

team out of this situation that is bad. For us to

understand the fact that God is in control, we must keep our faith and be mentally tough. I think that being mentally tough is a major asset to have in every group. God expects us to be mentally tough in order to get through the hard times. Life is not easy all the time, but we must be on our knees daily in order for God to help us in the bad times.

<u>Chapter 5</u>

Together we stand,

divided we fall

In this game called life, it is especially important to stay together in bad or tough situations. I have seen teams or groups disband or implode when things get rough. Mental toughness can and will play an important role in life when it involves your team. My mom always told me that they lived by the saying together we stand divided we fall, and it has a lot of truth to it. My mom also taught the same thing to us as we were growing up. To be honest, I am a very firm believer in that saying. No matter what situation your group or team that you're in, keep God first and stay together because sometimes being an elite group that can stand their ground may make all the difference rather you can get through the rough and hard times or not.

In order to stand together as a group, you must stand your ground. It is like the late great Malcolm X said, "A man who stands for nothing will fall for anything". This is one of my favorite quotes because there is a whole lot of truth to it. In this world you must stand for something. My mom always told me if you are right about the situation and you know it in your heard stand on it. Standing your ground is particularly important as a team. When you back down you start to show weakness and your opposition will take advantage of it. Sometimes when you are the leader of a group, you must stand your ground the most, because your group is counting on you.

Life is a Team Game

Backing down is a form of weakness. The example that I like to use is when you are playing a sport and you are hurt the opponent takes advantage of it and capitalizes. What I am saying is that you are not supposed to let the opposition know that you are weak. Like I keep saying you are going to have hard times while being together in in a group, but you keep asking yourself are we going to back down or we going to fight these battles together. It took me a long time to realize that God is in my corner no matter what the situation is. No hole is never too deep to climb out of as long as you have God in your corner, and when your group or team can realize that and be on the same page you can achieve anything in life if you set your mind to it.

God wants us to work together in life, but above all put him first. God is above all. It is like when you see teams competing for a Championship in sports, no one wins a title by themselves. The teams that won it had to take all the people that were involve accomplishing the common goal.

Standing your ground in a critical situation is particularly important. In order to make sure your team stays together you and your group must be men and women of integrity. Integrity is also an important asset to have in order to succeed. When you are a leader of a team integrity can be tough sometimes especially when people above you are in and out your ear so to speak.

Like I said before, hard times do not last forever that is why it is important to stay together. Staying together will help your group become stronger, and when that happens the sky is the limits and the team can have the willpower and faith to get

through anything. Also, remember God is in control.

Never have the divide and conquer mentality.

Some people may say that is the best way to go, but

in this game of life we are all in this together. When a

group divides or split, the chances of finding a good

direction in life can be slim. Sometimes we see

people struggling and we just turn the other way and

do not help them, God told us it is our job to do good

works by helping one another. Getting through the

hard times can be tough, but when the team or group

do it together that makes it worth-while. My mom

used to tell me and my sister stories about how her

and her siblings did things together. My mom was

trying to tell us divide and conquering was not an

option for them.

Sometimes, even if it is a team effort does not mean victory all the time. Losing together as a team is part of the game, but it is how you overcome adversity. When you or your team have that divide and conquer mentality, that does nothing but get in the way of the team's common goal. Everybody needs somebody in life to either talk to or to help them out at some point. When a person says that they do not need anybody that is not true.

An example I would like to use is basketball, if a person or the whole team is just playing for themselves it is not only selfish, but it is also bad for the team. Divide and conquer is not a good mentality to have when you are trying to achieve a common goal in this game of life. Like I said before everyone needs somebody. In my opinion, you only make it hard on yourself when you divide and conquer

because this game of life is not getting any easier.

Chapter 6

Never be Jealous of

another person's success

Well I am going to start this chapter by saying God is good all the time even in the bad times. Like I keep saying hard times do not last forever it is up to you and your team to change the current situation that you are in. God also saying that you can have an abundance if you just trust and follow him. Well what I am getting at is success does not always come easy. Hard work and dedication are two major assets to have.

I can recall a time when I was trying to get my driver's license when I was 19 years old. I was nervous about the test and the first time I took it I

failed. Back in the year 2010 I failed it again and I never tried until seven years later because of this fear of failure I had in my heart. I talked to my preacher about it and he told me do not be afraid, because he was going to help get through it. To be honest, I was afraid to ask some of my family members to help because of what they would say.

I realize for me to get my license I had to overcome the fear that was in my heart and also not worry about what people had to say about me. I mean I would always get it thrown in my face a certain female that I was talking to at the time and she would say that I didn't have a car or my own place at the age I was at during that time.

I remained steadfast and didn't listen to her nor did I let her discourage me at all. I told myself that God is in control. My preacher and I were a team

in this situation. The year 2017 came and I took the test and passed it and it was the one of the greatest days of my life. To be real, I was happier when I got my license than my first car. I did not worry about that female anymore or anyone that was doubting me.

In my opinion when most people doubt you that mean they can be a little jealous. Jealousy is an ugly and hateful trait to have. You would be surprised of the people that is jealous of you and your group accomplishments. Sometimes even your own family can be jealous of you, and what makes it so bad is that they may have more than what you have. It is like my mom would say it's not what you have it's how you treat people.

When a person that is part of the team is getting more attention or either getting more praise for his or her hard work do not envy them. Everyone

has a season to be great if you trust in the good Lord.
God teaches us not to be jealous or hateful toward
each other in the group or team that we are a part of.
In the bible, it clearly states that everyone and
everything has a time period under then sun.

I have seen people that was jealous of certain
teammates just for the simple fact that they are
getting more attention than they are. My advice
would be do not be mad at them embrace it your time
is coming just wait your turn. Having patients in life
while we are working together to achieve a common
goal can be hard sometimes. Life is not always easy
at times, that is why we need to work as a team
instead of being selfish.

Being happy for a person on your team that
has achieved a personal goal without being jealous
can be tough sometimes. When one person is jealous

in the group it can create a domino effect can turn out to be catastrophic. Jealousy and envy are two of the main things that needs to be avoided or handled when you are either part of a team or group. One of the best ways to deal with jealousy is by being happy for the person that may be getting a little more attention and praise than you are. I remember I time when Michael Jordan won the MVP award and the Bulls accepted the award as a team during that time. This is just an example of how to be happy for your teammates. The technical definition of the word jealous is the feeling or showing envy of someone of their achievements and advantages. God does not want us to be envy of each other because in his eyesight we all are created equal.

In my opinion, no one is about the group or team because it takes everyone's contributions to achieve success. Some people in groups quickly forget that. In order to never forget that no one person is above the group or team, all the parties that are involved must have a clear understanding on what is going on and how everything is going to be and agree on it.

This game of life is not always going to be easy, but when jealousy starts to play a role in the group that you may be involved in, it makes it tougher. Be happy if a person has a better idea than you may have, don't be jealous because in the long run it can hinder or destroy a good thing for the group from the inside if you let it. When the team has that good foundation/team first mentality, nothing can break it apart.

You do not have to be on a team to be jealous in life. Life is full of blessing and lessons to learn, so being happy for the person for doing good is a must

rather it is your enemy or friend. You can block your

blessing by either being hateful to others or just trying

to out-do the person that you are jealous of. Listen to

the good Lord when he says your time is coming.

Gods is not going to bless you when you're being

hateful instead of being happy for your teammate of a

person that you may not like for whatever reason.

Chapter 7

Learning not to bring

down a person

One of the key assets to have in a group or
team is confidence for yourself and for the people that
are in your group or on your team. This game of life
is not easy every day, you must struggle a little bit to
get where you need to be or where you want to go.
You are only as strong as your weakest link. One
person struggles then the entire unit does, so do not
let your teammate struggle. As a leader, you must
keep the unit together no matter what the goal or task
are.

In order to be a good leader one of the main
things that you will have to learn is leading by

example. Leading by example can be a tall order sometimes, and the reason being is because times will no doubt get tough, but it is how you get through them. Keeping your team or group together is a must if you want to be a leader. I think I was always the shy type, but sometimes when times were critical then I knew my role in the group from experience of watching the people that led before me so I could carry it on into the group that I was leading at the time while I was in school. Sometimes, leadership can be a heavy burden to carry especially when the team is falling apart and doing their own thing. Having faith in your leader as well as the leader having faith in him or herself is especially important for the common goal at hand.

In Matthew 11:28-30 **Jesus** says, *"Come to me, all you who are weary and burdened, and I will* *give you rest. Take my yoke upon you and learn from me, for I am gentle and humble in heart, and you will find rest for your souls. For my yoke is easy and my burden is light."* What I am getting at is when you are the leader of the group, turn to **Jesus** for guidance. I will be real and straight up, being a leader can be hard sometimes. When you make a lot of tough decisions it is not for only you but for the group to. The thing that I am saying is when you make an important decision you have to think about the people that are also in the group with you and get their input on what the team should do as a whole.

Some people are born to be leaders, some are not. For the people that are reluctant to become a leader of a group but is forced into it, most of the time things start to fall apart and implode within the group. Leaders take most of the responsibly within the group. It can be overwhelming at times, but at the end of the day you have your teammates to lean on for support. Some people may be leaders, but when things get tough that is when your leadership skills gets tested in my book.

The words leader and confidence can go hand in hand when you're trying to steer your team or group in the right direction to achieve a common goal in life. A leader with faith and confidence is a major asset to have running your team or group. Confidence in your leader can make the person that is in that position can make your group a better one because of the simple fact that everyone that is involved is following the positive direction of the person that is in charge.

One of the major qualities that the group do not want the leader to have is overconfidence.

Overconfidence can be a bad thing for the group. The right amount of confidence can lead you in the right direction most of the time. One of the key things to becoming a good or great leader one day is to know your limits. It is like I said before if one member of the team is struggling then the whole unit will follow. Overconfidence leads to cockiness and that is when the term arrogance come into play. The technical definition of the term arrogant is having or revealing an exaggerated sense of one's own importance or abilities.

If you a leader that is arrogant all the time, then you are not a very good one. Arrogance can lead to getting the big head sometimes. When you have the big head mentality you tend to make key mistakes that may cost you and your team in the end. As and leader of a group when you make key mistakes that cost your group or team from reaching a common goal at hand the people below you start to question your abilities and character on rather you can lead them or not.

The whole moral to this logic would be, do not be overconfident because any given day people from another group or team can beat you or show you up. In my opinion, it is like praying to God for what you want in life. God do not want us to ask and pray for something and you don't believe that he will get the job done and in addition to that he what us to have faith while praying and being on our knees. When you pray without the faith that God is going to get the job done it will be in vain.

I recall read about Solomon in the Bible. All Solomon wanted was wisdom on how to lead his people and the good Lord blessed him not only with that but being the richest and wisest king that ever was. Being a leader does come with good and bad things sometimes. Getting through that bad times is one of the things that can test your true leadership as well as your integrity.

Another thing to do as a leader is bring a teammate back up. Do not ever talk down on them but help them get their spirits up and get past the situations that life has to offer to derail the group or team goals. Life is hard enough as it is, and the last thing that the group needs is a teammate that is down and almost out. It is important to have the discipline for the group to press on the next hurdle in this game of life.

Bringing a teammate back up can be a challenge sometimes, but in order to be successful it must be done. I remember when I was playing football in high school that one of my teammates talked down to me, but the thing that I did was stood my ground and decided that I am not going to take this disrespect off any of them. One of my coaches did not know what to say when I stood my ground by telling one of my teammates off. The problem with that was I was very shy and did not say a whole lot, but I felt like that day I must stand up for something. My head coach at the time always said bring your teammate up and make him a better player by encouraging him to do better in what he is struggling in. Everyone needs a little encouragement occasionally, even leaders of a group. The team also needs to be discipline so mistake will be at a minimum.

In my opinion, even leaders make mistake from time to time. It is important for everyone that is involved in making the goal possible to reach to learn from their errors. Within every group there is always that person that wants to come down on his or her teammate for messing up. Just remember, when you do come down on your teammate make sure that it is for a good reason not for show. I have seen in my life back when I was playing sports that teammates have disagreements and one of the other parties try to humiliate them in front of everyone. That is not the right way to handle a situation if you have the intention to disrespect someone in front of people.

If your intentions as a leader of a group or team are to hurt someone's feelings every time they mess up, then you do not need to be one in my book. There is a time and place for everything that needs to be done about situations like that. Some leaders abuse their power by belittling the people that are underneath him or her. It is important to treat your

peers with dignity and respect, because in the long

run it will pay dividends. Sometimes you need to

come down on your teammate as a leader, but there

are positive ways about doing that. In order to be a

great leader, you must understand what your group or

team strength and weaknesses are as well as your

own. Leadership can be a heavy burden sometimes

but done the right way can give you more positive

results more than negative ones. Trying to belittle a

teammate under you is not the best way to go and can

cause your team to question rather you are a good

leader or not.

In order to not bring a teammate down, you

must have a positive mindset about things. The

positive mindset of either a leader or a person beneath

one is a must. When you have a positive mindset, it

gives you the confidence to achieve anything that comes your way. A negative mindset can cause you or your team to have messy results when trying to handle certain things that come in the way of the common goal at hand.

Have a positive mindset and learning how to bring a teammate back up rather you are a leader or not can go hand in hand. For you to bring a teammate back up, you must have faith and trust in them because in life when it's all said and done, we have to count on each other and remain humble. God wants us to remain humble even when times are hard, and you feel all is lost.

A positive thinker can get a whole lot farther in life rather than a negative one. It is important to have that positive mindset to hope for the best but prepare for the worse. When you bring down a member of a group or team just to play big shot, you are not only belittling them in the process of doing that, you are an embarrassment to yourself. In my opinion some people do not need to have that leader responsibility when they are trying to abuse it in the process by either mistreating people or just making poor decisions overall. It is just like when you are at a job working and your boss make questionable decisions that could impact the groups process in a not so positive way. It is particularly important in my opinion to have a leader of your group or team that has very noble intentions. The definition of the word noble is having or showing fine qualities or high moral principles and ideas. Being a noble leader of a team is a must. As a noble leader, must have to have good ideas for the team to make it pass hard challenges that life has to offer. Being ugly to a teammate that messes up from time to time is not a very noble act. Like I said before everybody makes mistakes even leaders, but it is also important to learn from them, so you don't make the same mistakes over and over again. I think one of the reasons why they teach history in school is because we do not repeat it.

When you are a leader or the head person in charge, you must have a positive mindset. Your leader's mindset may play a big outcome on rather your team succeeds or fails. It can be hard sometimes because of the pressure of being a leader, but your group or team is counting on you as a leader to lead them in a positive direction. While in church the preacher has a responsibility to lead the group in a positive direction towards God. When you are a leader with a negative mindset, your group will not get extremely far in life.

Another thing that must be done as a leader is praying for your team as well as yourself. Prayer is especially important because we need God for guidance to get us through this life no matter what we are doing. When your teammate messes up pray for them, do not belittle or down them all the time. If you must hurt other people in order to feel powerful, you are an extremely weak individual.

Chapter 8

Husband and Wife

teamwork

It says in the Bible that the husband and wife are as one which means of one flesh. Having a spouse that is willing to work with you and be by your side is a must while being married. Marriage is not all about sex, money, control, greed. Marriage is about loving one another rather being rich or poor. Loyalty and respect are not one-sided with it comes to a marriage or just being in a relationship with someone. I have seen that some couples do not work out just because either one party is giving his or her all and the other not giving anything. You cannot be with someone that do not want anything out of life because before you know it, they will bring you down on that same level that they're on.

Rather being in a relationship or being married, at the end of the day it is all about teamwork. I believe no matter what you do in life, you need help especially when things get too complex and hard. Husband and wife have each other to lean on when the outside world is starting to get the best of them in certain situations. I often hear on Facebook that sometimes the wife or girlfriend don't want to listen and have a smart mouth about certain things but in reality, it's not about controlling a person, it's about listening to what the husband has to say on certain situations and vice versa.

It says in the Bible that man is head of the household. At the end of the day, it is not about controlling each other, it's about respect and admiration. Husband and wife are as one and should have the love and the respect for each other. Even though a couple might fuss and fight, but at the end of the day marriage is a thing that should be worked on daily. Sometimes, when you tell your problems to certain people, they like stuff like that just for the simple fact because they are unhappy themselves. Some couples in my opinion have the learn the fact that what goes on in the household stays there. People are going to hate either seeing you and your partner happy together no matter what, that is why things should be kept between couples only.

Me personally, I have seen couples and marriages get torn apart all because of people interfering in their private lives and at the same time they do not have a life themselves. I would never let anyone, or anything tear my home or family apart.

Even if you have got to get rid of some so-called
friends so be it. Never let anything or anyone come
between your partner or spouse. Sometimes when
your married, you must make sacrifices for the
marriage or relationship to work. You also cannot
have a partner that is selfish all the time either. I have
seen some people break up because one person is
doing it all and not getting anything in return. When
you are not getting anything in return, then maybe it
is a sign that you need to leave that person alone for
good because they are making it very obvious that it's
all about them not you. You cannot keep trying to
keep a person happy when you are miserable doing it.
Some people do not even care if rather their partner is
happy or not.

Being in a relationship for the sake of just
being in one is just plain crazy. Some couples just

stay in a relationship regardless how they are being treated, and one of the reasons may be that they think that nobody else want them. My self-esteem was a little low at one time because I was misled one way or another. My mom always told me that there is someone for everyone in this world, you just must go find him or her. I will not settle for anyone when I know my worth. Self-worth is particularly important when it comes to finding or looking for that very special person you want to spend the rest of your life with one day. I don't care how long it takes me, but when I do find that special person that I want to spend the rest of my life with, we are not going to be just husband and wife we are going to be a team and get through things together.

Communication in life is one of the key components that you and your team, group or partner will need to get you through. Another reason why couples break up is because of the lack of communication. When you are a couple and do not communicate, that's when marriages or relationships grow apart. Working together and not quitting on each other is also a test of will power that makes the relationship worth staying in. When God is a part of your relationship, couples can get through anything that the world throws at them. You will find out if your partner loves you like he or she says they do if or when hard times come up. People's feelings and hearts change when hard times start to happen out of nowhere. Sometimes, when feelings for your partner or vice versa change they do not be for the better. For the marriage to stay strong and together, you must be as a team to get through the rough and hard times no matter how hard they get.

Life is a Team Game

One way to have a good husband and wife team is by paying bills together. When you are married, you are one flesh. It is not about who's money or who bill that is. A married couple must have each other back when it comes to bills and things like that, because it is not just a marriage, it is a partnership to the end. For a marriage or a relationship to work, both parties must do their part do not shift all the responsibilities on one person. In my opinion, some couples do not last longer than others just because of one party is doing all the work and not getting anything in return, nor feeling like they are appreciated.

Making important decisions together is important in a relationship, because at the end of the day it is a team effort. When one party has an important decision to make in life, talk it over with your partner before the decisions is made because in the long run it will pay off. I have seen people make decisions behind their partner's back and the end results did not turn out well for them. Making important decisions together no matter what the outcome is can save you a whole lot of grief.

When you have God in your relationship, things can be a whole lot better for you and your partner especially if both of you are praising him in the good and bad times. God is the key to having a happy and healthy marriage because when you both read the vows to each other, you must mean what you are saying and know the meaning behind them. When a coupe worship God together, it is a wonderful and beautiful thing because God is love and love conquers all things.

Life is a Team Game

One of the most important things as a team to do while you are married is to love one another no matter what. Sometimes you might get on your spouse nerves at times or vice versa, but at the end of the day you all will be still married and years from now you all will both be laughing about it. Loving one another is a bond that no other man or woman can take away. Your spouse is also your teammate when it comes to worldly battles daily. The battles that you and your spouse deal with each day are test God put in front of you. The strong couples that allow God to be part of their live last the longest in my opinion. If a person leaves you over one disagreement or misunderstanding, then they had no intentions of being in it for the long-run anyway. One reason why relationship or marriages don't last longs is the simple fact because God isn't apart if it.

Me personally, if I were married, I would do my best to be a good husband and father to my kids. I would make sure my wife was happy and be there for her as well as she would be there for me. There is a lot of give and take in a relationship. Disrespecting your spouse when you do not agree with what he or she is saying or doing is not the way to go. You and your spouse are a team and suppose to work out things together no matter who was wrong or right in a certain situation. Never be disrespectful to your partner in public because both of you are representing each other, and by making one look bad, you are disrespecting yourself in the process. Loving one another and being there for each other rather the times are good or bad is what God really wants and expects for us to do. It is a wonderful feeling when you have God on your side while you are married.

Life is a Team Game

In addition to husband and wife teamwork would be listening and understanding each other during a discussion about certain things. Some couple end relationships just because of a small misunderstanding. Respecting each other, listening, and understanding one another go hand in hand. The reason why I say that is because, if you do not listen to your spouse nor respect him or her, how are you both going to achieve goals together. If your spouse has a problem with the things that you are doing do not disrespect each other, talk about it instead of holding it in because the longer you hold something in the situation can get worse from there.

It irritates me when the other party says that they are not going to listen and have a smart mouth about the current situation, and them they wonder why certain things do not go their way as a team. If you want to be successful, you must sit and listen to someone in this world. It is not about control, it is about respect, trust, and the admiration that you have for each other to get you both through the hard times and become a loving and strong couple. A loving, strong, and respectful couples cannot let anyone, or anything come between them. If you have someone that is willing to work as a team to achieve goals and help you with yours and vice versa stay with them. Marriage or being in a relationship is not all about sex, money, or materialistic things, it's all about loving, respecting, and being there for each other rather it's good times or bad one. Even when you are married or happy you turn to God for guidance because that what he wants us to do in every situation rather it is good or bad.

<u>Chapter 9</u>

Friend Teamwork

The true definition of the word friend is a person whom one knows and with whom one has a bond of mutual, affection, typically exclusive of sexual or family relations. The meaning of the word friend in my own words would be someone that's there for you no matter what the situation is, and also a person that's going the keep it real with you from the start rather you want to hear or listen to the truth or not. These days and time, you must choose your friends carefully because people have hidden agendas and you cannot read anyone's mind. My only true friend that I have is Jesus.

Friendship and teamwork can go hand in hand as well. The reason why I say this is because in order for you to have a good friend that wants to be involved in the success you both or trying to make happen, teamwork has to come into play. When it is just you in your friend, both of you must do the work, not put all of it on one person. I have seen in TV shows as well as movies that when it's two people working on a project, it's always that one person that does all the work and the other party doesn't contribute anything but at the same time he or she wants some of the credit. That is why I said in the beginning of this chapter that choosing your friends wisely is especially important especially when it comes to doing projects together.

When it comes to teamwork as in working with a friend or best friend, both parties should contribute. Sometimes when a person does not want to help out and be lazy while you do all the work, things can take a turn for the worse. The reason why I say that is because the other person make think that they are being used the whole entire time as in being taken advantage of. In order to be a good friend and teammate, you have got to keep it real from the start. Each person has always got to give effort and contribution.

Being a real and true friend is a key asset to have when it comes to a partnership. A real friend is going to tell you the truth, be there for you, and keep it real no matter what, even if you hurt their feelings by telling them about what they are doing is wrong. A real friend is not going to help you do wrong. If you have one of them friends that is going to do the things I just said, hang on to them and give them the same thing in return. When you are a real and true friend, you don't count the favors and the things that you both have done for each other.

I recall watching a movie from a long time ago called A Little Princess, and this white girl and black girl made a promise to each other that they would stick together no matter what happens. In my opinion, it was a good movie because that is what friends should do because even at the end of the movie, they both left the cruel place that they were living in together. I was a child when I first seen the movie, but as I got older and watched it all the way through, I finally started to figure out what the value of friendship was. I just thought it was fascinating on how both girls made a promise to each other to stick together no matter what, and they did.

Life is a Team Game

In this life you have a lot of associates, but very few friends, and the few friends you have keep and hang on to them and keep your circle small. You must be careful on who you choose to have a partnership with to. I'm not say that always having your guard up is a bad or good thing, just be careful on who you trust to help you on projects or things that need to be done to achieve goals in the real world. When a friend is being real and recognizes that something isn't right from the start, don't get mad at them, take their thoughts into consideration and keep your eyes open because if you don't, it might be the downfall of the things that both of you have been working on and put a lot or work into rather it's a project or anything that's important.

Another thing that has to come into play in order for you and your friend to be successful in the project both of you are doing would be making sure both of you are on the same page at all times. Being on the same page as partners is especially important. Things go a whole lot better the smooth when you are on the same page as a team. When you are partnered up with your best friend, you learn more about each other from his or her like and dislikes to things that you all have in common. Sometimes, working with your best friend on a certain project can take a toll on both parties.

Staying on the same page can be a slow progress, but when it is all said and done it will all pay off in the end. You must take your time to make sure that everything is in order. It is never a good idea to rush through things when both parties want positive results. It is just like God said in the Bible, good things come to those who wait on him

Life is a Team Game

In addition to having a good and true friend as a teammate would be listening to each other ideas on certain things. Partners do not always agree on the same things, but when both of you talk about it, that can be a good thing. Do not belittle your friend/teammate just because his or her idea sounds dumb. Maybe his or her ideas can improve the situation that is keeping the project you both are working on a success.

I remember how my mom and one of her best friends worked together to come and get me and take me back and forward to college. They were friends for almost forty years prior to my mom passing. They pretty much did everything together. I really appreciated what her friend had done for me overall, and he is my Godfather. Like I said before, a true and real friend will stick by your side no matter what and

likewise in return.

Chapter 10

Teamwork in the

Workplace

Having that team first mentality in the

workplace is especially important. For the workplace

to be successful you must have the word teamwork

come into play. I recall when I was in the third grade,

that we had this same team first mentality. The

example that I am going to use is if one person forgot

his or her homework our teacher would not give out

candy. If everyone brought their homework in, then

we all got candy. The whole moral to the story was

my teacher was trying to teach us to work as a team in

the classroom to get that candy. I mean my teacher

had a cabinet full of candy that everyone wanted to

eat, so it was very seldom that people forgot their homework.

In order for your workplace to be a success you have to learn at least three things, but it may be many more, but these are my top three that I am going to be talking about in this chapter. One thing that I will be talking about is learning to know that your crew has a common goal to achieve.

The second thing would be putting whatever differences that you may have with a coworker aside. One of the most important things you cannot do is let anyone or anything from the outside come in between the group's progress no matter what. Those are some of the main rules that must be followed in order to achieve a team goal in the workplace. You also must be up to the challenge for anything.

Life is a Team Game

One key thing to having success in the workplace would be learning that the crew you are working with has a common goal. This common goal could be anything from having more customer to having good quality in the things that the workplace is producing. I remember a time while I was at work and another department messed up and sent bad parts. I said well that is on them, but another one of my coworkers said we are a team, so if it affects one of us then it affects all of us. My coworker was right, we are a team.

It is just like I said in the previous chapter, we are all in this together, and if one person struggles then the entire team does to. It is particularly important not to take you eye off the common goals that have been set for the team or group. When the workplace is working together, you can get a lot done in the process. Sometimes, it takes time for everything to come together because people have different ideas about how to do things.

As a team, the workplace must know that there is a common goal that need to be taking care of. The entire workplace must know what are the common goals that can be achieved so everyone can be on the same page. In order to be on the same page, you must make sure the group is putting in the same amount of effort into the goal at hand. In a workplace, everyone's job is important. My mom barely missed work when she was working because it not only affects you, it has affected the people that are around you. I once heard a long time ago that no matter what decision you make not only affects you, it affects the people that are around you rather it is good or bad.

The moral of what I just said would be, be careful with the decisions that you and your coworkers make.

Another critical thing to learn good teamwork inside the workplace would be putting personal differences to the side. Putting differences to the side rather it be against your boss or your crew can be a tall order sometimes. When you are working with other crew members, you are not going to always get along, they are just like your siblings that you are going to fight with from time to time. For the workplace or business to be a success, you have to put those differences that you have with a certain person aside for the time being.

Never let your home life affect the way you work in the workplace. Leave your work problems at work as well as your home problems at home. Home and work problems do not mix in a business. It is just like for example a couple works at the same business, same shift and everything, before you know it the home problems start to the affect their work performance overtime. When that happens, something must give. Sometimes, it may result in one or both parties getting fired because they are both disrupting work progress and involving other people in the workplace.

Sometimes, for the business to be a success, you to swallow your pride at time because in the long run it will pay off for everyone. You also have got to make peace, especially when a whole lot is at steak during that critical moment in time. I mean you are going to have coworkers that you are not going to get along with, it is just the way it is. Working with other people is not always easy and smooth sailing. When you and your coworkers get along and get through things together, good things are going to happen in the long run.

One of the last things to remember when you are working together in a workplace is to never let anything or anyone from the outside come in between the progress the group is making. This last thing that I am going to talk about is one of the most important things to remember when you're in a workplace in my book. It's just like when you become a Christian for the first time in your life, there is all kinds of temptation out there in the world. God expects us to not fall into temptation, but sometimes we do and that's why we need to be constantly praying daily.

When people let the outside world invade their workplace, that can be a bad thing. The reason why I say that is because you never know what a certain person agenda is, especially a high-ranking person. That has why God warns us about the devil, the devil is out to destroy and take souls with him to hell. While you are in the workplace, it is important to know your enemy that comes from the outside to destroy.

Chapter 11

Learning to trust people

This chapter I will be talking about how and learning to trust the people that are in your group or on your team. One of the key recipes to a successful group or team is learning how to trust people. This is the driving force and key factor on rather your group or team can be a huge success or not. I will be talking about three of the main things you will have to learn in order to trust people. The first thing will be that you need to put the past behind you for the common goal that the group is trying to achieve. The second would be keeping your faith on your teammates in life situations. The third and final thing to consider would be trusting in your own instincts.

Football is about trusting your teammates. It takes all eleven guys on the team to scored and make it across the goal-line. It is the same way with life in general, God has put us on this planet for a common goal and that goal is to serve him. God also want us to trust in him all the time no matter what you are going through in life. It is just like what William Shakespeare says, "*All the world's a stage, and all the men and women merely players.*" God has a purpose for us all. The words true ant trust go hand in hand. The reason why I say that is because for you to trust people, you must learn to read between the lines and figure out what their true agenda is.

The first thing that I will talk about as far as trust the people that you are in your group or on your team is trying to put the past behind you so a common goal can be accomplished in the process. Putting the past behind you can be a tall order. Sometimes, you

be wanting to bring up the past before the group is

form, but when you know what is at stake you can't.

When you put the past behind you, that can be the

adult thing to do.

When you or your team is doing good, there

are going to be people in and out your ear that is

going to bring up your past. One of the examples that

I like to use is when a person gets out of prison and

trying to do right. The ex-convict gets turned down

wherever he goes, and finally when the time is right,

he or she gets a job. When that person gets that job,

people always bring up their past. In my opinion,

everyone makes mistakes and deserves a second

chance to do right especially when they are trying

their best.

When you get baptized for the first time in your life, you become a new creature and you have accepted Jesus in your life. God says when you repent and ask for forgiveness, he does remember your sin any longer. The point that I am trying to make is do not bring up anybody past when there is a common goal to achieve together. Life is too short to be unhappy all the time because of the past that you or your teammates be bringing up against a person just because you or other people do not want to work with him or her. You do not have to like the people you work with, but you do have to respect them. Respecting your teammates and trusting them can be the difference between success or failure.

Keeping your faith in life situations is another thing that I am going to be talking about in this chapter. Everyone knows that life can be tough. God did not tell us that life was going to be easy all the

time. It has easy to say that you have faith when

things are always going good rather it be financially,

or you just blessed with material things. God puts us

to the test each day of our lives. You really get tested

when all the stuff that you have gets taking away

from you. You cannot be saying to people do not give

up on me when you have already given up on

yourself. It is you do not believe in yourself, then who

will believe in you. God wants us to work together in

this game of life by keeping our faith in ourselves as

well as each other. Praying before you and your team

start working on your goals in life is a must. God

wants us to ask and pray for things as well as each

other. Adversity is always going to be part of life,

there is no way around it. You are not always going to

be successful, but if you are scared to fail then you do

not deserve to be. Keeping your faith in yourself as well as in your team is a must to be a great success.

My mom used to always say that when you wake up in the morning it is a blessing from God. You and your team have got to always think that someone situation can be worse than what you are in, that is why keeping your faith in life situations is a good habit to have. When you learn to trust your teammates and have faith in them, your situation will not all that bad. Adversity can be overcome you just have to have faith and trust in yourself as well as your teammates that God will get the job done.

The definition of the word faith is having complete trust or confidence in someone or something. For some people it is ridiculously hard to have trust and faith in someone or something. One of the reasons being is because they have been let down so many times be certain people in their lives. The words fear and faith can go hand in hand sometimes because we are often afraid to trust, because the faith we done had in that person is gone. It seems like with some people once you lose their trust, it can be near impossible to get it back.

When working together in life no matter what you and your team are doing, you must trust each other for the group to achieve goals together. It is just like basketball, when the ball is moving and the team is working together to score, it is can be a beautiful thing to watch or play. Life isn't going to get any easier, you and your team will have to overcome adversity when times get hard. No matter what rather your group is in a good or bad situation, praise God.

God is good all the time, no matter what you and your team are going through rather its good or

bad. I remember meeting a woman and her faith was so strong in the Lord that it really amazed me. Sometimes, we forget that God is always in control, and has the final say so in the outcome. Keeping your faith in key situation is a must if you and your team want to be a success. It takes a lot of will power not to give up is certain situations in life especially when you are a leader of a certain group. It is like my mom used to say when there is a will there is a way. There is always a way to overcome the adversity that life has to offer as well as the temptation. God warns us about temptation and the results of it. I will be the first to admit that trusting people can be hard sometimes.

Trusting in your own instincts can be a challenge sometimes, but in some cases, it will have to be done sooner or later. That is why God gave us five senses that we can use. You have got to do what is right for the group or team that you are on. God did not give us five senses to waste, but he to use wisely. When it comes to trusting people, you have got to trust in your own instincts at the same time. Common sense can come into play when you know that your teammates or leader of the group do not know what he or she is doing.

Chapter 12

Being a team player in a positive way

When you think about it being a team player in a positive way is very much important. It is not only very important; it helps set the foundation for the group or team that you are involve it. The reason why it sets the foundation is because the whole entire team must come together as a unit to achieve anything that comes in the way of their success. Success is never given to you. When your group starts to come together as a unit, it is a beautiful thing, it is like poetry in motion so to speak.

The importance of being a team player in a positive way can and will come into play more often as you think. Every team needs that certain person that is willing to bring that positive vibe to the table. When you have a positive vibe, it can only make things better for the team. You cannot have a teammate that is negative all the time, it can a will destroy a team from within. When you are a leader of a certain group, you have got to do what is best for the team rather you like it or not.

Mistake are going to be made when there is group activity involved, and that is why it is important to have that good positive team player in your corner to make light of the current situation that the group is in. Learning from your mistakes is very much important when working together on a goal. The reason why we need to learn from our mistakes is because we will not have to worry about repeating them in a crucial situation. Like I said before, everyone has flaws that they need to work on. One of the main things to learn when you are a team player is to have that mentality that the team is always first. I have seen this in the NBA or NFL first-hand that certain players had to sacrifice things for the team to win a championship. You have got to make sacrifices in life in order to be successful and having that team first mentality is one of them. I have never seen one person win a football or basketball game by themselves, but I have seen a team that beat another team that had nothing but superstars on it.

God teaches us that anything is possible when you believe and have faith in him. When you have a good team and good teammates that have the same drive and goal to succeed, the sky is the limit so to speak. You cannot have teammates that only think about themselves all the time either. Being a good and positive team player can be hard sometimes because you always have that thought in the back of your mind that the goal is too hard to accomplish. I remember that there were times that I wanted to give up while I was in college. I kept going and everything and eventually graduated because I believed not only that God will get the job done for me, I also believed in myself.

For God to help you and your team in life, he wants us to believe and have faith in ourselves in the process. God knows what it is meant for certain people and he also knows when the time is right for things to happen. Sometimes, it only takes one person to hold the group together however, it takes a team to stay together.

Chapter 13

Being a part of the solution

Being a part of the solution rather than the problem can be one of the many tools that will determine if your team be successful or not. In this chapter, I am going to be talking about certain ways to be a part of the solution. Being a part of the problem will not help the group's cause in any way because when one person is being so disruptive, it can also turn into a distraction that will destroy a group from within. The last thing that a group or team needs is a distraction that is going to tear the unit apart.

There are many ways to be a part of the solution other than the problem. I am just going to talk about the main three in this chapter. There is always a solution to every problem that you will come across in life. Finding a solution to every problem can be a challenge sometimes, some people take on the challenge, and some people just back down. When you and your group are working on a project, all the sudden there is a certain problem, try to find a solution to solve it together.

God wants us to come to him with our problems true enough, but he wants us to help ourselves to. God always says do your best a he will do the rest. You have got to believe and have faith that the job that you want done will be done. It is like I keep saying, no matter what you and your group are going through in life give God the praise. Being a part of the solution to a problem can outweighs the alternatives. When you are working in a group it is not about individuality anymore. Being a part of the solution to a certain problem can also create more trust between you and your teammates.

One of the ways to be a part of the solution is to agree on some of the same ideas to achieve a common goal your group or team may have. In order to make that happen, you have got to have meetings and open discussions about certain ideas for the problem that needs to be solved. For example: it is kind of like when you are in a science fair and the teacher ask your team what your hypothesis is, each team member must come to an agreement in order for the project to be a success.

Agreeing on some of the same ideas as a group can be a challenge. Achieving goal together as a team not only builds trust, but also adds more chemistry in the long run. You have got to have that trust built up for the group to start agreeing on some of the same ideas. Each member has got to agree on the same idea. It also can be helpful when the group is willing to talk about the current situations that they are in before taking the necessary actions. Leaders of a certain group must learn to listen to the people beneath him before acting.

You never have to agree on every idea that comes up. Weighing the options out as a group and talking about things can also help. Lack of communication can mess up a group's chemistry overtime. It is very much important to have that communication window open because you do not want to have confusion within the group. When you have all this confusion about certain ideas, it can create a lot of bad things for your group. Being a part of the solution does involve you agreeing on the same ideas that the group may have.

Respecting another person's idea can be a tall order sometimes. That is what discussions are for when people have good ideas that can help the group or team. The more the group discusses the problems together the better off the group will be. When there is a lot at stake, keeping your mouth shut during that time came be the turning point on rather your group succeeds or not.

Another way to be a part of the solution is to contribute ideas. Ideas can come from anywhere, and as a leader of a group, you have got to have the people that are involved to carefully analyze them. Having a good idea that can help the situation needs to be disclosed to your group as soon as possible. Disclosing ideas with the members of the team or group can be a major help when they are carefully analyzed. In my opinion, when you have an idea that may can help your group, it is necessary to pray about it before taking whatever actions that are needed.

Never make fun or try to belittle someone that has an idea that can help improve or better a certain situation that the group may be in. I have seen groups disband and implode just because on person's idea had gotten made fun of. A misunderstanding and lack of communication can break up a group that is on its way to succeeding in life. A lot of members of a certain team that makes fun of a person's idea are usually the ones that sit back a never have anything that they can bring to the table. The whole moral to what I am trying to get across is never make fun or belittle a person just because they may have an idea that isn't relevant especially if you are one of them people that don't bring anything to the table.

When you make good contributions to your team, it can be like poetry in motion. No one can do certain things be themselves, and that is why we got to have good contributions coming from each team member at all times. Never let someone that is in the group taking up space to belittle your ideas just because they never have anything to bring to the table. It is very much important to stand your ground and not be afraid to disclose anything that may help the group you are in. Stay confident in your ideas, because when everything is all said and done, your idea may be the deciding factor on rather your team on your team's success or failure. Pray to God about your ideas because he can give you signs on what to do and not to do in certain important situations in life.

Life is a Team Game

The third way to be a part of the solution would be to get everyone in the group involved. When you are the leader, you have got to take on the responsibility of doing just that. Sometimes, when you as a leader, getting everyone involved can be a challenge however, it has got to be done if your team is going to be a success. Leaders of a certain kind of group have a lot of responsibilities when it comes down to it. You must get the whole group involved to be a success because as a team, you all are going to need all the help you can get.

Being a part of the solution to a common problem can make thing go a little easier for you and the people that are involved in the group. Never have people that is sitting around not doing anything or making good suggestions to improve the situation that the team is in. When some members of the group are not doing anything to help the cause, they are nothing more than a liability. A liability that is involved in the group can bring the whole thing down if you let him or her do that.

Never become a liability for anything in life, because if that happens groups, teams, or the workplace will not have any use for you at all. If you intentionally become a liability for your group or team, you are becoming part of the problem. This is one of many reason on why it is important to get everyone involved in order to achieve goals together other that certain people doing all the work and the rest are just reaping the rewards for things that they didn't contribute to the group or team. It is like I said in the previous chapter, it is not about individuals because at the end of the day the group is all in it together. Always have that team first mentality no

matter what.

Chapter 14

Poisonous Teammates

You have the teammates that are on your team that are good and got that team first mentality, but also you have the ones that are selfish, arrogant, and just down-right bad for the entire group. I will be talking about different ways to point out poisonous teammate when it comes to working as a group. You can easily point them out, it is not so hard. When you have poisonous teammates, it is best to get rid of them because if their actions are not corrected, they can destroy the entire group from within.

As a leader, you must do what it takes to win no matter if you must let a person go. Usually, when a leader lets a person go it is because they are considered as that poison that can break up and cause the group to be in total chaos. Chaos and turmoil are the last things that are need in a group. That is why being a leader of an organization can be a challenge sometimes, because feelings can get hurt in the process of the group success.

The true definition of the word poisonous is causing or capable of causing death or illness if taken into the body. In this game of life, you must learn the difference between a great team player as well as a poisonous one. Sometimes it can be hard to tell if a person is poison to group or not. When you are a leader, you must take on that responsibility of making sure that the group is up to par however, it may take a long time to figure out if a person is bad for the team or not. Like I said before, team chemistry is important for the group the be successful in life. For the team to be a success, the leader has the have that mentality that he or she cannot let anything from within nor the outside will destroy the group.

One of the ways to know if you have a poisonous teammate is when every time something does not go their way, they be the ones that is always complaining nonstop. When you have a person that is constantly complaining and being so negative all the time, it is time to either give them an ultimatum or just cut them loose. Cutting a teammate loose for any reason can be a tall order however, it also can be justified.

You can also point out a bad teammate by their actions. Well what I am getting at is for example when a person starts to turn teammates against each other, this is an example of how cutting a person loose from a group can be justified. When that certain negative teammate brings division within a group, it can destroy it if anything is not done about it. One of the last things that the group needs is a person in their own group wreaking havoc.

You may have heard the old saying that one bad apple can spoil a whole bunch. That saying is true when you are talking about a negative teammate. You cannot have negativity within a group and expect to be successful.

The whole purpose of being on a group or a team is to work together in order to be successful in life. You do not need all that negativity that has the potential to destroy a group on any given day. A leader can only do so much, that is why it is up to the rest of the team to keep it together and point out the bad apples that is causing the chaos and giving off negative energy.

A person that is giving off a bad vibe can also be a poisonous teammate. When you are forming a group or team in life, it is best to surround yourself with people who have a positive vibe and have that desire to win as much as you do. Winning is not everything however, when you have people with that same positive vibe as you, it is all worth while. When you have a person that is poison to the group, they are part of the problem. As a leader, you must handle a person like that in certain ways that you see fit.

One other way to justify the fact that you as a leader is trying to cut a person loose would be letting them know before hand if they are not trying to contribute anything that can help the team. Everyone must do their part in for the group to reach new heights. You cannot just have some people doing all the work while others just being lazy and complaining. In my opinion, that is why we have leaders to take responsibility in making sure the group is working together as a complete unit. Most of the time there is justification on why leaders let certain people go that claim to be part of the team however, they have not did anything let alone contribute to the projects that the team or group may be working on.

It may be hard sometimes to let a person go, but in the long run as a leader the group will be in a better situation because of the actions and sacrifices that the leader is willing to make for the team. A leader must make sacrifices for the best interest for the group. Leaders do have to think about what is always best for the group. I have seen coaches get rid of some of their best players just because they were thinking about what is best for the team.

When you have poisonous teammates, they can take a toll on the entire unit and cause the team to implode. That is why leaders must watch out for teammates like that. It is bad enough if the team gets destroyed from the outside, but when it is happening on the inside, it is a possibility that the team will never be the same again. Trust within the team or group is a major and important asset to have.

When the team lose trust in each other, it is only a matter of time that the team will fall apart. It is best to get rid of the bad apples that are corrupting the team. Like I said before, one bad apple can spoil a whole bunch. Bad teammates are nothing more than a liability for a team that is trying to achieve a common goal. Leaders also need to let any and everyone that is involved with the team know that if you are not going to help or contribute, then there is the door.

The words toxic and poisonous go hand in hand. The reason why I say that is because both words can and will destroy a group or a team from within. The true definition of the word toxic is something poisonous, or something very harmful or bad. When you are a toxic person that is trying to belittle the people that are a part of the same group that you are, in my opinion it is best that the higher authority to get rid of you. Being a toxic person is never a good thing, it also brings out a dark side that people do not know anything about.

Well I guess what I am saying is that when you have someone that is just wreaking havoc in a group, you have to part ways with that person. Parting ways can be tough however, like I said before their behavior can justify the reason to get rid of them. Doing the right thing and doing what is best for the team can be hard sometimes, but at the in of the day it is in the best interest for everyone that is involved.

When you are a part of a team and you have people that are toxic and poisonous, go to the higher authority to see what can be done about that person. Sometimes when you talk to that person that is causing trouble within the group, you may can change them. Talking to that person before you act is that best way to handle any situation that has the potential to ruin a good thing that is going on within the group. The last thing you want to do as a part of the higher authority is bring division from the inside. Each person that are involved with the group or team has a job to do, some jobs may be more important than other. If one person is not contributing or doing their job, then maybe it is time to have that one on one

conversation with them first before you as a leader

take any kind of action against him or her. When you

have poisonous teammates, they need to be

confronted about their action before it is too late.

<u>Chapter 15</u>

Staying together after the common goals are achieved

Well in this chapter I will be talking about staying together and looking out for one another no matter what. Life can be a beautiful thing if we all learn to work and stay together as a family. Like I said in a previous chapter when you are working together and looking out for one another like God expects us to do, life can be so much easier; and it is like poetry in motion so to speak. The longer you work with someone or a group of people, you develop a bond that no one from the outside cannot break.

Life is a Team Game

Before the team can start working together, you must learn to build trust in one another.

The four main keys that I will be talking about in this chapter as far as staying together when the job is done would be giving God the praise, never rub anything in your oppositions face, congratulating one another, and never brag on yourself for selfish glory. The things that I just mention above are four of the main things to remember it you want to keep the group or team together. Like my mother always told me, when someone helps you, help them in return because you never know you might need that person again in your life.

It is important to look out for one another even when the goal or job is done. We are all in this game of life together, rich or poor no one is above the other in God's eyes. God wants us to work together in this life. Life is not always easy; you might need a shoulder to cry one or just someone to talk to one day rather you are rich or poor. Life can be tough sometimes, but God always wants us to give him the praise no matter what.

The most important thing that the group must do when the job is done is give God the praise. God is above all, and God is love. Giving God the praise rather good or bad times is a must. God is good all the time even during the dark days that you and your group may have. The world may turn their back on you, but at the end of the day God is always there and in control of every situation in your life.

I recall when I was in high school that when it was game time we prayed to God. No matter what the outcome may turn out to be give God the praise, because when you have God in your life all things are possible. Without God, your team or group will not get extremely far. For your group or team to become a big success, one of the main foundations that you and your team will need is faith in God and each other. Building that important foundation is the most important thing that you will have to do for your team to achieve goals together.

God wants us to remain a team once the job is done and giving him the praise afterward is a must. Do not just pray when things are going wrong in your life, God wants us to give him the praise all the time. I could be rich and have all the money in the world, but it would not mean anything if I did not have God in my life. You can have all the money in the world and never be happy. I have seen rich people that have all this money and have a bad attitude just to be having one.

Jerrell Gooden

No matter if you are rich or poor, no one is above God, that is why we need to give him the praise no matter what you and your teammates are going through. Life is hard enough however, if you and your team can remain steadfast God will open new doors for you in your life that no one can close.

Another one of the keys that I am going to talk about is never rub it in your opposition's face. On any given day anyone can beat you. I have seen teams or groups that were so arrogant and cruel to other opposing teams. Your team can only be on top for only so long, that is what it is always important to stay humble and act like you been there before. Sometimes for young people it can be hard, and that is where self-discipline comes in. When you are taunting and insulting your opponent, usually it can add gasoline to the fire. It is never a good idea to taunt, insult, or underestimate your opponent at any time.

Always remain humble no matter what. God always wants us to remain humble and put him first. God also can bless us; however, he can also take your blessing away by blocking them when we are not doing what he tells us to do or just be arrogant. You and your group are only as good as your opposition. Rubbing it in your opposition's face can lead to problems. Always remember what it took your group to get where they are right now, never forget where you all have come from.

When you are on a sports team it is hard to get to the championship let alone win it all. Remain humble even during the darkest times and God will bless the team to get where it needs to be. As far as winning the championship is concerned, no one does it by themselves. I have seen a team that did not have any stars beat a team full of stars. What I am trying to say is your team or group may be good, but at the end of the day it is all about who wants it more. The team that wants it more usually becomes successful in the end because they either remained humble in the thickest fight, never disrespected their opposition, or just had the will and the where with all to remain steadfast in the darkest and hardest times.

In addition to this chapter of key things to follow when the common goals are achieved would be congratulating one another that was a part of the group or team. I have seen teams congratulate every one of their teammates for the success they have achieved together, and to be honest it is a wonderful feeling when that is done. When everyone is being acknowledged for what they have done as far as the contributions are concern that can be a wonderful feeling. As a leader it is important to thank the people and your teammates that got the group where it needed to be no matter what the project was.

Paying tribute to your group success in extremely important. When you are working as a team in life, everyone needs to contribute something no matter what it is. For the people that did not help or contribute anything, they do not deserve credit. As we give God the praise on what he does for us in life, we should do the same for the people that helped and stuck it out until the end. Life is no joke when you are dealing with certain issues on and daily basis. When you have someone or a group of people that are ready and willing to go bat for you, you must tip your cap to them because they did not have to stick around that long.

I think some of the best teammate that I have ever worked with are my family. That together we stand divided we fall saying is very real. When things start to get hard and tough, you really find out who your real teammates are especially when you are facing adversity. Even rich people must face adversity; there is no way around it. Some people struggle worse than others at times, and in this life, you are going to have them hard times.

Hard times do not last forever, that is why it is up to you and your teammates if you want to stay in the same rut or try to find a way out of the situation. Giving each other paise on a job well done is a must in my book. If nobody can recognize what you have done in life as far as making it better for yourself and your team or group that you are working with God does.

Life is a Team Game

The last thing that is an important key to staying together when the job is done will be do not brag on yourself. In other words, never get the big head. There is not any need to brag or boost on yourself and the team because other people will do that for you. Life is not about trying to outdo or out people. We were all put on this planet for one reason only and that is to serve God. When the group finally accomplish the goals, there is no need for all of that bragging and being arrogant. Arrogance can lead you into making careless mistakes, that is why it is important to remain humble.

The example that I am going to use is winning a basketball game. If you win or lose, it is important to show good sportsmanship. I have seen teams that refuse to shake the opposition's hand simply because of shame and pride. Having pride has its pros and cons also. It is just like I have always heard perception is reality. You do not want to be labeled as a sore loser. Integrity is a good asset to have rather you are a leader of an organization or just a teammate. In my opinion for a person to become a great leader of either an organization or just a small group of people, he or she must show that they have integrity and also the courage to either stand their ground or stand on what they believe in.

I have seen even the worst team beat a great one. Bragging can become an achilleas heel if your team let it. For the team to stay on top, you and your team must remain humble and have respect for your opposition. It is just like the late great **Dr. Martin Luther King Jr.** said, *"The true measure of a man is not how he behaves in moments of comfort and* *convenience but how he stands at times of*

controversy and challenges."

Chapter 16

Final thoughts

This chapter is going to be a recap over everything that I have talked about in this book. At the end of the day, life is a team game, and we are all in this together. For the team or group that you may be involved in to be a big success, you must know the true meaning or the word team. You also must define the word team in your own words. Some people may have a different definition of the word team however, at the end of the day it is all about the team and the common goals that you all are trying to achieve together.

God wants us to be a team. That is why it is important to put God first in everything that we do in this game of life. You are going to have your stumbling blocks, but never try to limit yourself in what you can and cannot do. Where there is a will there is a way. God will make a way out of nothing just when you think all is lost. Keeping your faith is a must if you and your team want to be successful in life.

Learning about one another can be a challenge sometimes, but for the team to come together, it must be done. When I first started working, I had to learn some things about the people that I was going to be working with. It was tough sometimes because I was quiet and shy and did not say much. Sometimes, you must adapt and adjust to change for you to fit in.

Like I said in a previous chapter when you work together as a team, life can be so much easier. For everything to fall into place, you must develop a bond that no one from the outside can break. Some people can naturally have good chemistry with people however, it may take others some time to develop that team bond that no one can break. You and your team must also stay focus on the goal that is at hand. Your group or team is not always going to be successful, but if you are scared to fail then you do not deserve to be. Everyone needs somebody at some point in their life.

You are not going to get through life without any help. When you are selfish and all for yourself, you are not going to get extremely far in life. We as humans should lean on each other rather than trying to outdo one another or down the next person. I have seen other people down the next person just because of the way they either look or act, but God expects us to help people when there are down and out. Rather you are rich or poor, we all are equal in God's eyesight. We are not any better that the next person.

You really find out who your friends are when times get tough or hard. Choosing your friends wisely is a must. I am going to use an example as far as the team breaking up. When a certain person gets kicked off a sports team the whole team wants to just give up; when they do that, you all were not a team to be begin with. The moral to that example that I just used would be never let a person from the inside break or destroy the team's chemistry.

One way that you and your team may be judge is how to get through adversity. Adversity is one of the main tests in life that God puts before us. God can test our faith and trust in him in many ways. It is our job to not let the devil come in and take over. No matter where you go or what you do, take God with you. God wants us to love him with all our heart, soul, strength, mind, and love your neighbor as well so yourself. No matter what you are going through keep your faith and trust in God.

Never envy or be jealous of your neighbor. In this game of life, you must learn how to be patient. Being patient can be a challenge when you are young. There is a time and place for everything. Everyone and everything have a season. It says in the one of the books in the Bible called **Ecclesiastes chapter 3** versus one through eight and I quote, *"There is a time for everything, and a season for every activity under the heavens: a time to be born and a time to die, a time to plant and a time to uproot, a time to kill and a time to heal, a time to tear down and a time to build, a time to weep and a time to laugh, a time to mourn and a time to dance, a time to scatter stones and a* *time to gather them, a time to embrace and a time to refrain from embracing, a time to keep and a time to throw away, a time to tear and a time to mend, a time to be silent and a time to speak, a time to love and a time to hate , a time for war and a time for peace."* I recall having a conversation with my mom about certain things, and all she told me was to be patient it is not your season yet. With me being young at the time it was frustrating, but as I got older, then I was beginning to have a better understanding on what she was talking about.

Having and keeping a positive mindset when it comes to working together is one of the major assets to have. You must always think positive and make light of the situation for the team or group to be a success. It is not going to be easy all the time. You and your teammates are not going to agree on the same things all the time either, that is why communication about certain ideas that can help the team is the key.

All the chapters that are in this book are basically some of the building blocks on how life can be for us sometimes. In these chapters, they also talk about how to handle and do things as a team. I often see people comparing one athlete to another, but at the end of the day it takes a team to win a championship. No one can win a championship by themselves, and that is when that trust and faith in your teammates come into play.

Leadership can be a heavy burden when it comes to leading your group or team to victory. Success does not come easy because there is always somebody that is better than you. One of the leader's main responsibilities would be to keep the team together when there are hard times.

I think when two friends stick together during the good times and the bad can get through just about anything that life throws at them. You really find out who your friends are when you are going through tough times. If a friend cannot or is not willing to be there with you when times are a little hard, then you may want to ask yourself was he or she your real friend all along. Some people do not know the real meaning of the word friend until it is too late. Friends are supposed to help each other and be there for one another, not one person that is doing all the work. A real friend also does not count favors either. You have a lot of associates in life, but you have very few people that you can consider to be your friend. When you have a good friend that is willing to go bat for you, hang on to them and likewise for them in return.

Life is so much better when we all work together. Trying to outdo one another is not the answer. God tells us to do for others and expect nothing because, we have our treasures in heaven. Life can be beautiful, especially when we learn to work together. The choice is yours if you want to be miserable every day or happy. Sometimes, God pull us out of our comfort zones to test us for example the ice storm in the year 2009. We all had to come together during that time. God just wants us closer to him, he can do anything to get our attention even if it takes him causing a natural disaster to do so.

Sometimes in life you must work with a person that you do not always get along with. You must make the best of the situation that you are in because that word pride can cost you and your team in the end. Do not let the pride get in the way of the team's common goal. Sometimes you and the person that you do not get along with must put the differences aside to achieve a common goal.

Like I said before, for a team to work together as a complete unit, the word trust must come into play. Trust can be the deciding factor on rather your team succeeds or fails. Faith and trust are two of the main things you must have with God as well as your teammates for you to get to the next level in life. Without faith and trust in God, you are not going anywhere in life.

In this game of life, you also must watch out for certain people that do not bring or contribute anything to the table. No matter what you and your teammates are doing, no one is too good to not contribute. When everyone gets involved and helps, it is like poetry in motion. You win as a team and you lose as a team. That is why it is best to get everyone involved especially when the stakes are high.

When it comes to teamwork in the workplace, everyone's job is important. If one person is struggling, then the entire team struggling. Helping the person that is struggling is extremely critical when it is crunch time. As a leader of a team, it may be frustrating to help the same person that is struggling all the time however, in the long run you will be glad that you did not give up on him or her.

The world is not going to get any easier or better; so that is why we must look out for one another. Do not play the fool either because some people want others to feel sorry for them. For God to help us, we must learn to help ourselves first. I am going to close with this statement, life is not easy, you will have your stumbling blocks that will get in the way. When you a person or a group of people by your side, there are no limits to what you and your team can accomplish. When you and your team are in the thickest fight, take the word of God with you. It is like what **Jesus** said in the bible, *"With men this is impossible, but with God all things are possible".* Amen.